Visiting the Minotaur

for Andrew, Daisy, Sophia,
Mick, Jake & Milena

Visiting the Minotaur

Claire Williamson

Seren is the book imprint of
Poetry Wales Press Ltd.
57 Nolton Street, Bridgend, Wales, CF31 3AE
www.serenbooks.com
facebook.com/SerenBooks
twitter@SerenBooks

ISBN: 978-1-78172-443-9
ebook: 978-1-78172-444-6
Kindle: 978-1-78172-445-3

A CIP record for this title is available from the British Library.

The publisher acknowledges the financial assistance of the Welsh Books Council.

Cover artwork: 'Alexandra & The Minotaur', Oil on Canvas by Matthew Grabelsky
www.grabelsky.com

Author photograph: Catherine Hawkridge

Printed in Bembo by Airdrie Print Services Ltd.

Contents

Swimming with the Bull

The animal is bookended by two women
floating on a Cretan wash of silicate copper,
their blanched skin soaked into walls
by hydrate of lime.

Their black curls, carbonaceous shale,
ripple down slim topless torsos,
same as the man in haematite
somersaulting the back of the beast.

The athlete's body mirrors the whip
of the tail, an inverse curve
of long horns clamped
under feminine biceps.

Anklets, bracelets, vibrate with energy,
the bull complicit in this dance
tucks in his choreographed head,
eyes intelligent, body curving like a dolphin

plunging through three-and-a-half-thousand years:
an earthquake, eruption, tsunami,
the rising myth of Atlantis,
so that I'm swimming next to bovine hide,

pulled through the labyrinth's two thousand rooms:
potteries, banquet halls, wine presses, shrines,
all stamped with the sign of the bull.

My Brother and Mother as Horses

They sit at a green plastic table
with me after all these years,
enjoying a pot of tea in May sun.

I stand up to pour,
ignoring that they are horses.
How else would they return?

My brother still wears the blue noose,
now loosened like a hippy necklace,
drawing attention to the deep-ridged cuts
under his chin, like a tree trunk sawn
by an amateur. I try not to stare.

I couldn't grasp hold of the rope
with these hooves. Once I'd jumped it was too late.
He waves them about, knocking
his teacup out of its saucer.

I grab a napkin, mopping up,
No use crying over spilt milk.
A silence follows –
lit by the white flood of his skin
shining through close-cropped hair.

My mother, a blood-bay, is shy,
her forelock flopping over her forgive-me eyes.
I say, *I'd love to see more of your face.*

She thrusts her black muzzle
into the cleft of my torso and arm
and I feel her warmth for the first time
since she drank that poison.

Her trembling mouth
tugs the highwayman's hitch in my ribs
which I've had since she left me
three months raw to the world,
chewing my thumb to its bone.

That knot which I've pulled tighter and tighter
lets go with a slip,
a fall.

They both reach out to catch me,
but I'm the only one with hands.

The tea set wobbles
as if a steeplechase is passing.

If I Have Time

for PC

You could be sending me a postcard right now
from your hotel room, following a Picasso exhibition
in Seville. You could be scurrying off
a three-page letter on file paper, not sullying the card,
so I could keep it, would keep it.

Your letter would suggest a coffee, if I have time,
in the Rainbow Café in Clifton, sharing a quiche and salad
on a shaky metal table in pavement sun. You'd tell me
about your screenplay, peeling back its skin,
pithing the plot.

More than twenty years of correspondence
sits in a ring binder. Your commentary on my writing,
my life, your stories. When I was grieving my brother's
early death, you said, *It's autumn, you're rotting.*
And you were right. Knew me like a father

should know his daughter. If I had time,
I would meet you for that coffee, but I'm so busy
knowing it's too late for your words. Knowing that scene
of my life has passed. Your screenplay lies unfinished.
The exhibition has closed.

On Guernica's 80th Anniversary

for the people of Aleppo, Syria

Even the light has sharp edges,
slicing an arm that, like Psyche,
illuminates truth.

A mother's breasts exposed,
neck bent in a guttural howl,
catching the bull's breath
as she cradles her dead baby.

Eros is missing
where severed horse legs lie,
fingers still clutch a snapped dagger.

Mouths awe at the sweepings of people,
eyes melt from faces,
arms flung like flames,
burning alive in a black box.

Hear the mare's shattered whinny,
as the mirror drops
on this broken city.

Brizzle

A country schoolgirl, I ran into Bristol's arms
lovesick, August ninety-one, freedom drunk
on DJ Jazzy Jeff and the Fresh Prince.
Summertime in a Broadmead shoe-shop
where the Ritzy girls found their perfect pair
in leopard print platform brogues, reflected
in patent boots that reached under tartan minis,
like the river beneath the city centre.
Back then I didn't know what it was
that stopped me from spinning out of control,
like cars rounding St James Barton after midnight.
I now know I was grateful for everything, even
the concrete Bearpit, Dingles' dated department store,
Park Street's gradient, a choice of glass-strewn dance floors.

No Man's Land

The relief midwife
    cannot make eye contact
        with me, the meat
on the narrow slab
of the hospital bed.

She says, *It's like the Somme,*
        as if today's cut
            has no ears.

In my personal trench,
    I spell out a name
        to keep my senses.

I'm losing blood,
    every gasp of gas and air, a decision:
        do I give in to the pain,
           grinding pelvis and spine,
               stop breathing in protest?

I start to pass out
    on a white battlefield,
        hearing distant screams,
    while I grab my nightie,
scrap of dignity.

        Until she holds up my child,
           bright lights blinding above me
               in a place called No Man's Land.

The Minotaur Speaks

Today I walk near the threshold,
sun on my pale muscles, horned head
heavy. I can barely raise it.

No need for a door
to this maze. Shame
has been my gatekeeper.

Every seven years,
seven petrified children
rot in the clammy dark.

I knot their discarded clothes
around my hooves,
so they don't hear me.

I only lick the lichen.
I don't touch a hair
on their Minoan heads.

They eat each other in the end,
caught in hunger's fists,
not knowing they aren't me.

Daedalus was the architect
of this labyrinth
and my mother's infidelity,

creating a cow disguise
to hide her while my father,
the white bull, had his way.

I lean my cheek on stone,
notice something
that makes my tail twitch

for the first time:
a boy with burning wings
is falling from the sky.

Certificate

Canada would be
coated in a cot sheet of snow,
tight and smooth to the corners.

She would need a passport, of course.
The first step, to order
her birth certificate.

Childish excitement
in her sixty-year-old fingers
as she folded the request, cheque,
stamped-addressed envelope,
like the origami of a babygrow
doubled into a letter.

When the document arrived,
she recognised her own writing
on the package,
but not the strangers' names inside.

She shouted into the misted window
where her mother used to stand

but nothing came back,
not even an echo.

Her ancestors stretching
into distance, faceless as ice.

Vernix Caseosa

I'd read accounts of babies
unprepared for this world:
slippery, fishlike, alien.

You come covered in thick sebum,
waterproof, an astronaut,
confident of inner-space, outer-space
this planet
        and the next.

Survivors of Bereavement by Suicide

After the group we chatter on the sleeted pavement,
warmed by the details
of our shared stories, coroner's courts,
how our separate deaths
found their way into news reports.

Someone comments on conversations
overheard at work, the banality
of clothes, shoes, what so-and-so said
to whom. And I perk up
to offer my truth.

How I long to find comfort
in the cut of a skirt, pleasure
in the tucked pleats of a jacket.
Experiencing what the eye likes
will be a sign of life.

And this very conversation we're having
about 'them and us' is a gaudy
hand-crocheted scarf, beanie hat
and matching gloves, knitted
by a well-meaning aunt,

separating us from the cool set.
Every clashing colour
tells our confidential histories,
our own brand of gossip
about pills, hangings, drownings,
fault, guilt and blame.

It's a fashion we never thought we'd wear,
but we wear it all the same.

Cows

They flick the weathervane
of my heart.

Sometimes through pink-tinged mist,
sometimes in lemon light,
their Friesian presence radiates
sheen of black, cream of white.

Soundlessly, breaching the gate of morning,
the herd spreads out
and with pleasing spacing
writes ABC for cow
on a clover-green page.

Spilt-paint breath
splatters aluminium air.

Split coffee-bean prints
liquefy frost.

Breastfeeding

On the one side
it feels like
I'm being sliced
with a scalpel as ever-soaring
scales of pain
pull piglet-squeals
from my throat.

On the other side
your operatic fingers
reach up to my breast
and stroke the way
a maestro might
caress the air:
there-there
there-there.

Fruit Machine

At age twelve my family became a gamble:
grapes, apples, melons kept spinning,
refusing to find their kind. I'd watch combinations

match on my friends' reels: grans, uncles, parents,
the similarities in their eyes hitting the jackpot.
I smacked 'nudge', 'hold', kept pouring in coins,

until the unexpected cascade into open palms,
a full sibling, aunts, cousins, my bloodline
burnished like a row of cherries.

On Not Being Able to Write about
a Dog without Sounding Sentimental

The antique fur coat
she throws around her shoulders.
Long hair plaited,
sprayed stiff to a baton
to conduct her mood.

She lets deerstalker flaps
fall to her cheeks.

Silver evening gloves pulled past elbows,
she folds her fingers for paws.

Onto the carpet she slides her belly,
rolling in the open curtain's sun

to bask in the opera
of her growling dreams,
legs twitching
against the pace
of an orchestral heart.

Only stirred by the tink
of a dinner dish,
crinkling plastic.

Bakery, 1986

Shooed out of the house to buy a loaf,
I rush to the bakery on my undersized bike.

The queue curves round the shop
like a croissant. I check my watch.

Looking at the encrusted loaves,
I can taste the dry crunch of poppy seeds.

On my fifteen-year-old chest,
the scent of swelling dough settles my breath,

a comfort not felt at home. I wait,
squat as a bap, among the adults,

observe them through the slanted mirror
that doubles the stock of cottage loaves,

their dusted buns tied tight, matronly,
decent as my stepmother.

I notice a young woman, face risen with curiosity,
hopeful as buttered crumpets.

The queue shuffles forward,
exposing terracotta tiles

and me, that same young woman,
I don't recognise.

Unimagined Mother I

I don't imagine you
just out of reach, as Lara,
me as Dr Zhivago banging
on the tram window.

Nor lost in a crowd
like Mario Ruoppolo
swamped at a political rally,
never making it to the podium,
your unvoiced poem trampled.

You're not Susie Salmon observing
from her omnipotent heaven,
trying to break through
to send messages in coded light.

Nor Banquo's ghost,
taking Macbeth's seat
at the table, whose *absence*
lays blame upon his promise.

Deep Winter

Hunters in the Snow by Pieter Brueghel the Elder, 1565

How cosy it feels for you to come home to this village triangle.
Houses glow gold, despite their snow roofs, echoed
in pitched mountains across the valley.

Fire-lit, a thin fox drapes down your back,
tracked by a drift of dogs that snuffle
the ground for morsels. The inn sign slanted

in disrepair, familiar as the skaters on the ponds:
black, slick, escaping the weight of snow.

On the soothing 'm' of the bridge, a figure
shoulders a bundle of sticks longer than this day,
which threatens to close early in a raven's wings.

Bathurst Pool

July-hot at the lido.
You screech, as at each metal step,
cold water laps higher up your chest.
I watch. *Can you touch the bottom?*

Cheeks puffed out
you let go of all
that holds you,
except my eyes.

As you sink,
the water breaks
with the tips
of long strawberry plaits.

Thin arms trail like rushes
failing to crown the surface.
Your apple-face blurs –
no nose, no mouth.

I peer down, the seconds stretching
into our drowned future.
How long will she be?
Come on.

Too late to call the lifeguard,
I jump in beside you
and take hold
of your small body.

My dress billows
on the surface,
then clings, as your in-breath
pulls us gaze to gaze.

Bill

We walk past about 9pm, see the door off the latch.
Dave from over the back has discovered you
naked on the carpet,
staring wide-eyed at the ceiling.

Your house has been turned upside down
like a bar-room brawl,
splintered stool, papers everywhere.
No sign of a break-in.
Dave's wife's calling an ambulance.

I kneel by your head
where the bath towel covering your body
halts. I get you talking,
stroke your thin arm,
bring back those old conversations –

how you hunted rabbits, showed me your war photos:
you, handsome and assured in uniform, not
this skinny bruised man on the floor,
with a black eye and broken nose.

Over and over,
you're trying to strap
your watch to your wrist.
The catch is tricky,
I help you fasten it.

This is not just a fall.
You've been searching
for some other time
all evening long.

In Our City Lives

my daughters and I
would not have taken
a stroll past bedtime.

We wouldn't have left
by the back gate
along the right of way,

seen the peacock's teal ballgown draped
over the fir-tree branch,
damp linen smell of feathers,

witnessed his chicken-like flap
as he climbs the tree's staves, unable to unzip
his rustling dress before bed.

We wouldn't have discussed
bird-boys and boy-boys.
How bird-boys put on a show

like girl-girls in prom-wear,
not like bird-girls
in their plain suits.

We wouldn't have climbed
our staircase to bed, lumbering
with the weight of love,

dreaming of boys in taffeta
and girls in tux.

Rough

One evening, she took her teenage body
beyond her step-parents' five-bar gate,
to the sixth form college,

where she'd grown a little more
into her skin with Shakespeare,
Chaucer, Eliot as friends,

to the tennis court where she curled up
on a bench in her thin coat. Slept.
Woke to sun backlighting the conifers

across the churned-up hockey pitch.
A voice, wearing a mother's dress,
persuaded her back:

We almost rang the police. Almost.
The officer might have asked
why she'd rather spend the night
alone, sleeping rough,
than be in bed at home.

Matryoshka

With her rosy cheeks,
headscarf, wide hips
and hint of glitter;
with her painted-on lips,
that beatific smile,
a twist of carefully carved wood

reveals, with a squeak,
another version,
diminutive, plainer,
lacking the outer sparkle
that helped him choose her.

He saw someone capacious
to take on his babushkas.
She only had room for herself
in ever-decreasing depth.

I unscrew each nested outline,
until I reach the beige
unvarnished core, small enough

to swallow toddler-like.
A kernel that won't crack,

can't bear offspring.

Mříčná, Czech Republic

Rumbling in zigzags as if they're my daughters,
two roe deer with sturdy cherry branches for legs
gallop past us to jump flower borders
in neighbours' back gardens.

Behind the house, four storks follow a tractor,
bamboo limbs synchronised, models on a grassy catwalk,
wearing black-fringed monochrome shawls,
turn their bodies, beaks, necks into lines,
and rise towards the pine forest.

Rumours circulate the village,
reports of a broad-pawed wolf
taking sheep on the Krkonoše Mountains,
while packs roam the Polish border
licking their lips.

Characters known to my children
only in storybooks from libraries
pop-up, land in their laps.

Soap Opera

Thick black lines
redact your words
and your name, mother,

masked
like kidnapper's gaffer tape
in a cheap TV drama.

When the others
take their parts,
they stumble on gaps
in the script
made by your absence,

pronouncements
not quite adding up
without you.

They plough on –
the ratings slump.
An invited audience sniggers.

And here I come
running into the studio
with the bright lights

bouncing off my features:
your liquid eyes,
your aquiline nose.

Some of the characters,
uncomfortable,
shuffle up grumpily,

while other actors
embrace me
off-set.

Perspectives

Las Meninas by Diego Velázquez, 1656

In the Royal Alcázar of Madrid
paintings crowd the walls
like applicants, barely
inches apart,

with Infanta Margareta Theresa
centre stage, her dress a galleon
on which she floats
between *las meninas* –

ladies in waiting,
one offering deference
the other sustenance –
while her parents, freshly oiled

in Velázquez's portrait,
watch from the mirror's copy
as they sit for the painting, beside you –
yes you, the viewer –
to see Nieto, the valet, pause on the step,

his hand pushing back the curtain,
uncertain whether to go or stay –
although, as the artist knows,
he's framed at vanishing point.

The Walk

'1384: It is a hundred years since our children left.'
Hamelin Town Records

Without a goodbye, my children were led away
through a crack in the Prachov Rocks,
too narrow for adults, and were gone

while I
scrambled a scree, crossed a bridge
to the next valley, to find them safe,
comparing boulders on the trail,
unaware of my frost-splitting panic.

I've been thinking of Hamelin.

Not the piper dressed in jester-scarlet,
hunter-green, whistling rat songs along
the River Weser. Not him.

But rather the mothers who gaze
through streaked kitchen windows
at sandstone stacks.

And I think of that old painting
showing a teardrop-walled town on a rainy day,
dwarfed by a high hill cleft open
with a muddy, rock-filled landslide,
ready to crush the town's youngsters,
while the settlement's red roofs
stand stiff as open prayer books.

In the same picture, fathers punt, fish,
oblivious to the imminent disaster.

I think of that ripping yarn –
a limping lone survivor-witness,
vermin and betrayal –
told and retold,
which won't be written down
for a hundred years,
explaining how it can possibly be,
that as quick as the flick of a rodent's tail,
we can lose our children.

Unimagined Mother II

I long for you privately
to buy me a surprise red winter coat
with roses round the hood,
to love my daughters,
have them on your mind.

For me to make you lasagne:
soak the pasta strips,
mix the white sauce
until free of lumps,
serve it bubbling, triumphant.

These secret longings
comfort me when my girls are away.

One unexpected gift
is my confidence that mothers,
even absent mothers,

are forever mothers,
however distant, however dead.

My Daughters Blueberrying

Under the troposphere of spruces
blueberries are mounting
patiently in the pail –
small hands turn maroon,
work with the rhythm of ants
on pine needle hills.

Palms of ovate leaves
gather licks of rain.

On low bushes
the fattest fruits are highest,
plump with yesterday's sun;
they smudge lips with temptation,
lure pocket-sized fingers
closer to earth.

Beyond the Abstract Face

for PC

We never went to Barcelona together.
We never went anywhere
beyond Clifton and Bedminster's cafés.

On this visit to the city of Picasso and Gaudí
you stand beside me, talking
about Pablo's quick sketches, a *picador*
flashed out in a few strokes
to the quivering point of his lance,

how Antoni extrapolated nature
with ribcage arches,
snail-shell cupolas,
a reptile staircase.

You taught me to see beyond
the abstract face of things,
to believe the feeling
arresting the imagination,
as ideas become real, visual, visceral, tested.

You travel with me,
your death releases you
to be in two places at once.

Stepmother Minotaur

Carnivore breath on my neck,
cold nose ring numbing my cheek
reminding me that nothing will be easy.

She kicks me in the small of my back
to choose the stoniest route,
the steepest climb.

I've made friends
with the fleas that thrive
in her fur, each one a critic –

a symbiotic parasite.
I'm so familiar with their tricks,
I've learnt how to make them leap

so, I walk through each door
a little lighter, despite shouldering
the Minotaur, and those times
I've mistaken myself for her.

After the Coming of Darkness

for JL

We sit in the Royal Albatross Centre café,
with its panoramic windows,
on the tip of the Otago Peninsula.

You're a teenager,
I'm your estranged aunt,
a poor substitute for your dad.

We're warming up
as relatives and from our coastal boat trip,
eating scones, drinking tea,
very British, very Pākehā.

I smile at your genuine interest
in marine birds, the albatross
we spotted above the Pacific Ocean.

It feels like we're on the edge of the known world.
For a few seconds
you are your father, my older brother,
and I'm twelve-years-old
giggling with you about something

that doesn't concern itself with death,
a feeling waddles up between us
like that blue penguin chick, *korora,*
active only after the coming of darkness.

Extremities

The explorer on Radio Four describes how men
climb mountains because they can't give birth

and be mothers, how time and heat
are crucial for Alpine adventurers.

I imagine a scattering of climbers
blurred like birds on a cliffside.

Caught alone in a blizzard,
one has lost a leg below the knee.

Frost has bitten off another's fingers and toes,
five days trapped in an avalanche.

I want to call them all home.
They shed extremities, while I gain

ten carabiner toes dabbed dry
in a white towel's snowstorm,

looped arms slung around mine
in the crevasse between sleep and wakefulness,

thighs which gripped my waist in infancy
clamp on five years later

preparing for cols and peaks
on the ropes of my time and my heat.

Distance

for PD

One day you woke, sensitive to the light,
and decided it was time to take the books back.

You marched them –
Nietzsche, Ricard, Rilke, Valéry –
down through that wet town
to the second-hand bookshop,
wiping tears from your freckled cheeks
with the heel of your palm.

You told the puzzled assistant
you couldn't cope any more –
would she take these books
off your twenty-something hands?

I know you miss
those dead wise voices,
loyal companions for so long.

Looking back, you're sorry about the distance
between your bookshelf and the shop,
the friends you gave away,
loving everything, even us, in retrospect.

She Thought Her Father Was a Butcher

watched him smash the arched roofs
of the carcasses into chops,
then line them up
with parsley in the shop.

She could have hidden under a pig,
breathing in the dry smell of blood,
but she preferred the white-tiled corner
where she could watch

the butcher she thought was her father,
his right hand a cleaver,
his left a poker-shaped sharpener,
attacking the skinned animals
whose pink flesh was as plump
as her forearms.

But he would never hurt her.
She was his daughter.

She thought her father was a butcher,
but he was not her father.

Laika

A stray dog from Moscow's streets
became the name
on the world's lips,

a rising star circling
the earth in Sputnik 2,
a one-way trip.

Not much is heard of her backups,
Albina and Mushka,
just Laika, meaning 'the barker'.

They were all tested in the centrifuge,
trained to eat space gel,
confined in ever-decreasing spaces.

Yes, there was love:
Yazdovsky who took her home
to play with his children;

the technician who kissed her nose
before the hatch was closed.
Her heart hardwired to the spaceship,

for three hours she was weightless,
pulse racing, but ate her dinner,
alive to see an orbital sunrise.

Heterotopias

When I sat, aged twelve,
on the brown and orange sofa
where she told me I was not her child,
I was also outside in our garden
with the neighbour's forbidden black cat
stroking his back all the way
to the tip of his tail.

When she backhanded me
in the hearse-like Volvo
because I bought the wrong dog food,
I'd already slammed the car door,
was walking up the wildflower borderland
of the road, wiping my bloodied nose.

When I left the carving knife on the table
with the back door unlocked and she slit a mouth
in my cream jumper, cut my skin,
I was already topless, the discarded garment
staring up at me with its caked red lipstick,
which I'd never be allowed.

Temple Church, Temple Street, Bristol

1. 12th Century Round Church

My heart is a circle, a promise from those who crusaded this sphere,
      twelfth-century knights approved by Jerusalem's King,
for pilgrims to travel unharmed, freely crossing frontiers
      in this mystical ring.

My name is a cross, blood-red on a habit's white swing,
      for monks who took vows, but didn't adhere
to the limits that poverty, chastity, obedience bring.

My light is a star, through each grilled shutter it peers,
      marking time, and the disorder this order will bring.
They will take my stones, but my spirit's still near
      in this mystical ring.

2. 14th Century St Katherine's Chapel: Martyr's Door

Speaking from the wings
like a Shakespearean fool,
a weaver has the measure of it:
Fie on this idolatrous worship.

Like a Shakespearean fool,
a hypocrite is in the church,
fie on this idolatrous worship.
Pointing the finger

a hypocrite is in the church,
burned as a heretic
pointing the finger
in flames on St Michael's Hill.

Burned as a heretic
a weaver has the measure of it
in flames on St Michael's Hill,
speaking from the wings.

3. 15th Century Tower

Leaning five feet
 out of the vertical.
  When my bells rang,
   I swayed, and they say
    that boys hid walnuts
   in the splits of my
    masonry, using me
     as a giant cracker.

    After the bombing,
   soldiers feared I'd
   collapse, placed
    dynamite at my feet.
   Locals saved me,
   saying, *It's okay.*
   She's always been
   slanting this way.

4. Late and Post-Medieval Holy Cross

My tower tilts like the mast
of a sinking ship on a grassy sea.
My body is a whale's carcass
beached on marshy Temple Fee.
I was hit in the Blitz and the fire
left little but bone walls that stand
upright as my congregation, my choir,
their echoes long-blown across the land.
My toll-bells clang high by College Green,
my font transplanted to another Holy Cross.
The wind and crows have picked me clean,
except some fronds of fungus and the moss
that grows like tiny tongues in sweet ascent,
those little lungs that breathe my gut's lament.

Atonement

My brother was never
the European Forest *toro:*
hide impenetrable
to arrows, blades, spears,

more petal-skinned, emotional like Nandi,
faced with divided loyalty
between his master, Shiva,
and his master's wife, Paravathi.

Honoured to be integral
to their dice game
that rolled on for years,
Nandi positioned as both prize
and umpire.

Despite heroic gestures,
my brother was caught
between guilt and shame,
each spiralling him downwards.

When the sport
tumbled to its conclusion,
Nandi favoured Shiva,
the loser.

Betrayed, Paravathi cursed the bull
with an incurable disease.

My brother thrashed,
a fish at the end of a line,
guts twisted, hooked on escaping.

Nandi in agony,
begged for a stay of execution
on his scab-patched knees.

Paravathi declared Nandi's atonement:
One day a year give up
what you savour most.

My brother savoured the prospect
of reunion with his son,
touching his muscled shoulders,
smelling his gelled hair,
hearing him play punk-drums.

Nandi chose judiciously
to give up the grape green grass
that surged his mouth with saliva.

Nandi was cured, relieved,
the next day, joyous,
chewing his delicacy.

My brother chose to give up
the taste of possibility.
Falling from so high, snagged,
even he was surprised
not to find his feet again.

Red Herrings

He left them everywhere, pungent. As a child
she tried to wash them, watching their rise and fall,
lifeless in the machine's rhythmic drum.
She pegged their pale tails on the drying line,
but they were still overpowering.

She bathed in herrings. He forced
them in her mouth at mealtimes
with his rhetoric of how noble he was
to take her, the anomaly, under his curing roof.

Herrings to slip on in the hallway
and to wear to the ball in front of his friends,
disinfected, glistening green, gaping, silenced.

She couldn't smell him and yet all the time
he was there, her own father, right under her nose.

Mummy Island (60°N, 147°W)

for my daughters

We look at the atlas
and find it, a twelve-mile
paddle from Cordova in Alaska.

Semi-submerged in canoes, we
are hybrids, half-women,
half-porpoise. Midway

we spot a black bear cub
on a grey beach inspecting
his claws, the arched love-heart

of his body. We pause
to watch him, oars on
our laps. Cavorting sea otters

catch droplets of light and pull
them into the darkness of the sound.
The womb of the inlet teems

with pulses, the minke's call
a volley of kisses, the humpback's
spiralled incantation. Islands

cluster like fir-trees, a family
of islands. We sit up late
to hear Chugach legends, our backs

against rocks, bathed in pine-scented
smoke. I bend forward to smell
your hair and close the book.

Blame

Again, that dream.
Always the same, but different.
Mutating.

My brother and I have killed
someone in self-defence,
but what is not defensible

is the relaid patio we circle.
The moment's passed for confession.
We both know it's only a matter of time,

tick-tock, exchanging knowing glances
in our stride, like the hands of a clock.

The dream recurs.   I'm alone.
Now it's my brother
beneath the flagstones.

The gas-lit forensic tent
is still as Midsummer's Eve.
Inside shadows overlap,

clumsy puppets
wearing Tyvek suits,
step down below the terrace.

Excavation, layer on layer,
a sunset of soil and silence.

This is the last night the dream
will come back.

How do I know?

                                        They walk out of the tent
                                        empty-handed,

shake their heads,
snuff the lamps,
dispose of plastic coveralls

to which nothing sticks

                                        not even blame.

Priscilla Jones

by Thomas Barker, c. 1802

She sees through him,
the artist, her betrothed,
to the backdrop of their engagement.

One glove removed: candour
or preparation for death?
Perhaps Priscilla suspects both,

wary of his motive
to build house, gallery, studio
on land her aunt owns.

Her upright torso
parallels the Doric columns
of his plans; the slab

of her cheek, a façade
struck by full sun
that will fall into shade

for sixteen years:
trapped,
she will never leave the house.

Her eyes slide towards
a future self
he'll never paint.

Labour

The night he stole three-headed Geryon's cattle,
Hercules slept through, exhausted.
The flame-breathed giant, Cacus,
not one to miss a trick,
jealous of the hero's bounty,
taught half the herd to walk backwards,
pulled reluctantly by their tails;
to leave no trace,
concealed them quietly in a cave.

And so it was with my birth family:
I slept for thirty years before
the herd of my bones
called out to their hidden relatives,
their footsteps erased from my history,
not found in mud, loam, sand or paper.

When the certificate bearing
my mother's name
inched nearer by post,
my skeleton ached to speak
like those abducted cattle
that sensed their ancestral drove
moving closer and began to low.

My spine bent to the spelling
of my matronymic line, as if in labour.

I Never Did Join the Circus, Did I?

I never became a silver-plumed high-stepping pony,
trotting around a ring in rhythm to climbing chords,
or a trapeze artist in a light-winking leotard
shot from a cannon, waving.

I didn't travel from town to town
with no fixed abode or juggle neon rings.
Nor did I walk tightropes between rigging,
jump through hoops blustering with fire
in the held-breath black.

I do stand in the twilight,
the only tempo the thud of jeopardy
sharing my firefly words with strangers
who clap and lift my wings,
hauling up the big-top of my body,
lighting it from the inside.

Tauromaquia

Of all the tools I could choose:
the *verduguillo* for the final stab,
the decorated *banderillas* to tear muscle,
the picador's horse vantage and lance,

I take the *capote de brega,* the fuschia overcoat,
folded for the grand *paseíllo*.

I shiver within brilliance,
surrounded by the cupped hands
of whispering spectators,
stand face-to-face with this creature,
remember how I used to cut up
a cow's tongue to feed my dogs,
scissors breaking against
its thick, ripe silence.

A toe inches forward. A snort.
I breathe in sweat,
metallic spit of flesh.

Exhale with a pink lunge,
throw the cape around his neck
with a daggerless hug.

He yields.
Like me, he never wanted
this dance of life and death.

We drown
in the crowd's collective moan,
thumbs down.

Our trembling knees,
bloodshot eyes,
meet in the sherry dirt.

The Spiral Staircase

I find myself thinking
     about reaching the top,
         attempting to climb a stair at a time.

        Wise enough these days
    to realise there is no
        skipping a step. Each tread polished,

        slippery, progress is tricky.
   My hands clamp the banisters,
      hoist this uncertain body.

   There are days
 when I put three steps skilfully
behind me, only to make a mistake

    and spend a week clinging to a balustrade,
      panting, as if on a precipice.
        I don't know what I will find

    when I reach the top:
      an ending, my feet,
        or the grief I tried to leave
          by the first riser.

Split Ends

We haven't played Mummy Island
for a while, but this morning you
sit on my legs in the bath, while
I wash your hair. I hold a flannel
to your eyes to stop the soap-sting,

tumble your towel for a minute
in the dryer, making it cosy,
fold your hair in a super
absorbent wrap. Turn you
and your sister towards the TV

to distract from the tugs while I
comb and dry your hair, pump
in serum for smooth ends.
Tonight, you will stay at Daddy's.
I always have that same feeling

of savouring this time, before
we're seventy-five minutes apart
for four days, eighty-miles-per-hour cars,
cross-winds, hard shoulder,
no rest-stops, the motorways.

At Yewberry House

The garden calls me outside,
pulls on its day clothes –
faithful grey jeans cold with grime.

Beyond the hedge's green jumper,
spooling threads of sparrows,
the cliff falls away like the plunge of bad news.

All in the past now. Like the dropped names
of the far fields, running free of house, road,
heading to the Severn, the sea.

On this outcrop –
no subsidence. Crimson licks of rose unfold.
I stand on the edge, tilt
to let this day catch me in its shabby arms.

Visiting the Minotaur

An extravagant daytrip
from Waterloo to Gare du Nord
with one purpose, to see
the Minotaur emerging from a cave
carrying a dead white horse.

He's a victor over domestication,
raising a palm in an arm's length gesture
to a veiled woman witness
on a fist of an island. He hauls
his conquest and burden,

limp legs dragging, hooves chipping.
One more step and he'll trip
on its wave of a tail, but not yet, not ever.

I sit alone in the gallery,
in front of twenty-four square metres
of gouache and ink, the very canvas
stabbed at, as Picasso's marriage collapsed.

I'm here because I am the Minotaur,
the veil, the hand, the island,
the woman, the horse, the hooves,
the cave, the fist, and the death.

Aknowledgements

Acknowledgements are due to the editors of the following publications in which some of these poems (or versions of them) first appeared: *Split Ends* (Eyewear), *Raceme, From Palette to Pen* (Holburne Museum), *The Cardiff Review, Elements of Healing* (Poetry Space), *Project Boast* (Triarchy Press).

'Rough' was Highly Commended in the Bridport Prize, by Lemn Sissay. 'My Mother and Brother as Horses' was awarded 2nd prize in the Neil Gunn Poetry Competition 2017 by Michel Faber. 'She Thought Her Father Was a Butcher' was Commended in the Poetry Space Competition, 2014, by Alison Brackenbury. 'Survivors of Bereavement by Suicide' was longlisted in the Aurora (Writing East Midlands) Poetry Competition 2017 by Penelope Shuttle.

'Unimagined Mother I' and 'Unimagined Mother II' were inspired by Carrie Etter's collection, *Imagined Sons* (Seren, 2014).

'Stepmother Minotaur' makes reference to the story, 'Before the Law', a parable within *The Trial*, by Franz Kafka.

'Temple Church, Temple Street, Bristol' was written for the Sanctum project, as part of The Spoke's Seven Stars contribution.

Thank you to Seren and in particular Amy Wack, for her close reading and encouragement.

This collection would not have been possible without the love and support of my friends, colleagues and extended family.

I would like to thank all the readers and mentors who offered advice and practical support: my colleagues of The Spoke (Paul Deaton, Elizabeth Parker and Robert Walton), Julie-ann Rowell, Katrina Naomi, Bob Mee, Jenny Lewis, Graham Hartill, Rhian Edwards, Richard Axtell and Clare Woodford.

Particular thanks for reparative friendships with: Jennifer Bhambri-Lyte, Sara Blake, Paul Curtis, Rose Flint, Catherine Hawkridge, Julia O'Connor, Julie Primon, Jane Sallis, Nicki Sellars and Eric Starr.